WALKS WITH CHILDREN
IN THE
LAKE DISTRICT:

PATTERDALE

Other *Questa* Guides, published and
in production

Walks with Children in the Lake District:
Buttermere and the Vale of Lorton
Borrowdale
Ambleside and Grasmere
Around Coniston
Keswick and the Newlands Valley

Walks with Children in the New Forest
Walks with Children in the Peak District

WALKS with CHILDREN
in the Lake District
PATTERDALE

Terry Marsh

A Questa Guide

© Terry Marsh 1994
ISBN 1 898808 00 7

Questa Publishing

27 Camwood, Clayton Green, Bamber Bridge
PRESTON, Lancashire, PR5 8LA

ADVICE TO READERS

Readers are advised that while the author has take every effort to ensure the accuracy of this guidebook, and has been required to revisit all the routes during the course of preparing the book, changes can occur which may affect the contents. The publishers would welcome notes of any changes that they find.

Also by Terry Marsh

The Summits of Snowdonia
The Mountains of Wales
The Lake Mountains: Vols 1 & 2
The Pennine Mountains
100 Walks in the French Pyrenees
100 Walks in the French Alps
The Dales Way
A Northern Coast to Coast Walk
50 Classic Walks in the Pennines

Printed by
Carnmor Print and Design, London Road, Preston

CONTENTS

EXPLANATORY NOTES

Introduction: Questa Walks with Children are intended to introduce young people to hill walking. They range from short, simple river or lakeside ambles, to fairly energetic ascents of fells, sometimes to a considerable height. The walks are not graded, but are intended for groups, with supervised children roughly between the ages of six and fifteen.

Only parents, of course, know just how energetic, determined and resilient their own children are, and so each of the walks gives no more than an indication of the distance to be walked, and the amount of ascent, not necessarily all in one go, you can expect to face. All of the chosen walks have been done with children, and children of all ages have been seen happily plodding along them - they do have remarkable tenacity and boundless energy at times.

But these walks aim to do more than give route descriptions. They aim to educate young and old alike in the interests of the countryside, and the history that surrounds it. So, with each walk a few brief notes tell you what you might find along the way.

Maps: Simple diagrammatic maps accompany each route description. These are based on Harveys Walker's Maps, a specialist map, just for walkers, produced on a waterproof material.

The maps in this book are to scale, either 1:25000 (2½ in to 1 mile~4 cm to 1 km), or 1:40000 (approx. 1½ in to 1 mile~2½ cm to 1 km). These should prove adequate, in good weather conditions, to guide you round the walks, but you are advised always to carry a more detailed and extensive map of the area.

It is recommended that you buy Harveys Walker's Maps if you wish to learn more about the countryside beyond the limited range of our diagrammatic maps. To cover the walks in this book, you will need the map for Eastern Lakeland, available in both scales.

Footpaths: Almost all the walks are on public rights of way, permissive paths, or routes which have been used over a period of many years by custom and practice, but any mention of a path does not imply that a right of way exists.

It is unlikely, however, that you will be prevented from following any of the walks mentioned in this book, but you are asked to stick to the paths at all times, especially where they are waymarked, or go through or near farmyards, to be sensitive to the work of the hill farmers, particularly at lambing time, and to keep any dogs you may have with you, under strict and close control at all times.

Equipment: It is important to go well-equipped into the fells, and for everyone this means adequate footwear and waterproof clothing. Small and growing feet will benefit all the more if footwear more substantial than wellington boots or trainers are worn, and will reduce the risk of slipping.

There are rough and wet patches on most of the walks, and for these you will find that modern walking boots with a cleated rubber sole are the best footwear. This remains true even during dry spells in summer: trainers, for example, offer no support to ankles, and while they might be adequate for walking along streets, they cannot cope with steep grassy slopes.

The Lake District, alas, is frequently wet, and a good waterproof should always be carried, along with an extra pullover, cardigan or jacket to compensate for the lower temperatures you will experience as you climb higher, or walk close by the lakes.

Warm trousers, not jeans (which are useless when wet, and offer no protection), are advised, though you don't need expensive walking breeches.

Carry extra food and drink, along with your waterproofs and spare clothing, in a small rucsac.

You must always carry a compass, and understand how to use it properly. If you wish to learn more about the skills needed for walking in the hills, you might consider *The Hillwalker's Manual*, by Bill Birkett (Cicerone Press).

Finally, remember to take with you the good sense to turn back if the weather suddenly changes for the worst.

Route Directions: All the walks start from a car park or convenient parking place, but do remember to secure your car against thieves. Keep valuables out of sight, and don't lock animals in the car without adequate ventilation and something to drink.

The directions given in the text are usually right or left in the direction of travel. Sometimes compass directions, east, west, etc. are given. It is on the walks in this book that children can begin learning how to read maps and use a compass. Never let an opportunity to do so go by.

Distances and height gain are measured, and rounded up or down. Distances are 'Total Distance' for the round trip. Height gain is not always continuous, but reflects the many ups and downs you will face.

KEY TO MAPS

The maps in this book are produced at two scales. One is the scale 1:25000, the other, 1:40000. Distances on these maps are represented as follows:

1:25000 (Walks 1, 3, 5, 7, 11, 12, 13, 15, 16, 17)

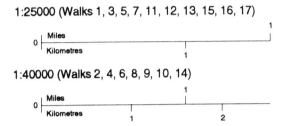

1:40000 (Walks 2, 4, 6, 8, 9, 10, 14)

The following symbols have been used on all maps:

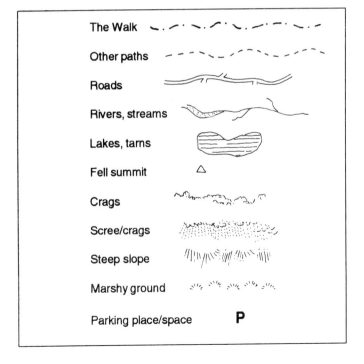

The Walk	
Other paths	
Roads	
Rivers, streams	
Lakes, tarns	
Fell summit	△
Crags	
Scree/crags	
Steep slope	
Marshy ground	
Parking place/space	**P**

PATTERDALE

"...an islet of population, a green ditch hollowed out of that alien world of mountains where plants and beasts and weather all behave as if they belonged, as indeed they do, to a world apart from that of men."

Days in Lakeland: Past and Present. E.M. Ward, 1929

There is a tradition that Patterdale is named after the Celtic St Patrick, one of three missionaries (St Ninian and St Kentigern were the others), believed to have visited this region on evangelical missions during the early fifth-century. The name is said to derive from St Patrick's Dale, but historians are not unanimous, and W G Collingwood, sometime Personal Secretary to John Ruskin, comments: "The legend...is unfounded that St Patrick on his wanderings through Britain preached and baptised here."

Another construction on the derivation of the name comes from twelfth-century records in which the dale is called *Patrichesdale*, a combination of the Norse word for valley and the Old Irish personal name *Patraic*. Since the majority of Norse settlers who colonised the Lake District came from Ireland, it is probable that the Patrick who gave his name to the dale was an Irish-Norse farmer from the tenth-century. Certainly, there is no evidence of a Christian base in Patterdale before the end of the twelfth-century.

Pursuing this religious theme one step further, it is almost certain that if indeed St Patrick had preached here, Patterdale would have emerged as one of the principal medieval parishes: instead, its early history is inseparably linked with the parish of St Michael's Barton.

Today forming part of the great county of Cumbria, Patterdale, before the reorganisation of 1974, was divided between Westmorland and Cumberland, with the former claiming the larger share, certainly of the countryside covered by this book.

Patterdale Hall evokes memories of days then the dale was ruled by its own 'kings', the Mounseys, though their royalty was self-styled. They were, nevertheless, acknowledged principals in the dale from the day their ancestor led the dalesmen in defence of their homes against Scottish raiders. This dynasty continued until 1824, when the Marshall family came to the Hall.

The old inn at Patterdale was a favoured haunt of a coterie of the so-called Lake Poets. Walter Scott came here, and with Wordsworth and Sir Humphrey Davy ascended to Red Tarn in 1803 to see the spot below Helvellyn where a faithful dog watched over the body of his master for three long months.

The Wordsworths were undoubtedly enchanted by the valley, and it was along the shores of Ullswater, at Gowbarrow Park that they saw the "crowd, a host, of golden daffodils". Dorothy noted: "When we were in the woods beyond Gowbarrow Park we saw a few daffodils close to the water side. We fancied that the lake had floated the seeds ashore and that the little colony had so sprung up. But as we went along there were more and yet more and at last under the boughs of the trees, we saw that there was a long belt of them [the end we did not see] along the shore...I never saw daffodils so beautiful they grew among the mossy stones about and about them." It was from these notes in Dorothy's journal that William composed his poem some two years later. In 1805, visiting the valley in November, Wordsworth himself wrote: "The steeps were reflected in Brothers-water, and, above the lake, appeared like enormous black perpendicular walls. The Kirkstone torrents had been swoln by the rains, and now filled the mountain pass with their roaring, which added greatly to the solemnity of our walk."

Today, the valley echoes to the throngs of visitors: ramblers, hill-walkers, motorists, cyclists, mountain-bikers, yachtspeople, rock climbers, day-trippers, and holiday-makers, swamping the resident population fifty-fold (I would guess). Yet Patterdale accommodates them all: it needs to, because its outstanding beauty, its history, its literary associations, will always draw the crowds.

For the walkers, with children, to whom this book is addressed, the length of Patterdale and is tributary valleys harbour a wealth of walking opportunity. This guide gives an eclectic selection, that seeks to contrast and balance easy lakeside and riverside walks on which children might first learn to understand and appreciate the countryside, its interpretation and its natural history, with some energetic and extended assaults on higher fells, to which you can progress logically, and without the objective and subjective dangers that attend many of the routes that are available.

At one extreme, children will happily scamper across Striding Edge, and consume a ten mile walk with barely a complaint. At the other, the indoctrination needs to be a phased process, encouraging by visual and physical satisfaction, rewarding with the pleasure that comes from achievement.

This book seeks to satisfy both needs.

WALK 1:
Brothers Water

The walk around Brothers Water is both delightful and easy, and on a fine spring or summer's day the perfect opportunity to have a picnic by the lakeside. The

Start: Cow Bridge car park. GR 403134
Total Distance: 4km (2½ miles)
Height gain: Virtually none
Difficulty: Easy; just take care with very young children while passing through the caravan site, and as the route touches the main valley road.

oak woodlands which flank the early part of the walk are very ancient, and host to an amazing variety of birds: wood and willow warblers, chiffchaff, whitethroat, pied flycatchers, redstart, and the occasional marauding cuckoo. Out on the lake you might see red-breasted merganser, coot, great crested grebe, cormorant and lesser black-backed gulls, as well as the more plentiful black-headed gull.

The beauty of the walk lies in the way it presents familiar views from a different angle, and takes you close enough to the high fells of this corner of Lakeland to whet your appetite.

THE WALK:

Leave the car park by crossing the stone bridge spanning Goldrill Beck, and turn left through a gate.

Just beside the gate there is a National Trust notice board, with an excellent illustration of the valley ahead, and an explanation of the way the valley was formed. It also contains useful information about the farming practices in the dale.

Set off on a broad track beside the beck, passing along the bottom edge of well-established woodland in which oak and beech predominate.

A small wooden bench, near the outflow from Brothers Water, is dedicated to the memory of Ted Hartsop, and presents a pleasant view through the trees into the valley of Hartsop, to Gray Crag and Hartsop Dodd. A small shingle beach nearby would make a fine spot for a picnic, were it not so early in the walk - but you can always come back.

11

Gradually the path rises gently, away from the water's edge, and cuts a swathe across the woodland slope, decorated in spring and summer with primroses, violets and ransoms, or wild garlic.

Once beyond the southern end of the lake, the path continues above broad alluvial pastures, formed thousands of years ago by deposits washed down from the surrounding fells. At a gate, keep ahead to reach Hartsop Hall Farm and Dovedale Cottage.

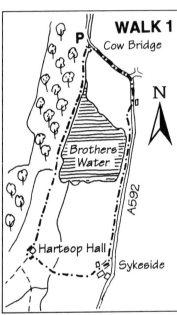

Follow the track past the farm, and, ignoring paths going off to the right, swing round, left, in front of the hall, and then immediately right across a cattle grid. The ensuing access track runs along a field edge to the caravan and camping site at Syke Side Farm.

Walk through the site to reach the farm buildings. Pass by

these, and continue to a Y-junction, with the Brotherswater Inn up on your right. Keep left here, and continue up the driveway until, just before reaching the main road, you can go left, through a wooden gate, and on to a stony path (signposted: Permissive Path to Brothers Water).

Soon the path reaches a gap in the wall above, and for a few quick steps skip along the road, immediately to descend a path to the lake shoreline.

Follow the shoreline, taking care not to trip or slip over many tree roots, and passing two more places where a picnic or brief halt might be in order.

The path gradually leaves the waterside, and rises to a gate in the wall alongside the road. Once through the gate, turn left, and follow the road back to the Cow Bridge car park. There is a grassy margin on the left side of the road, and a metalled footpath on the other. By the time you reach Brothersfield Cottage (dated 1781) you will need to cross the road to avoid banks of wild flowers growing in the road margin.

ALONG THE WAY:

Hartsop Hall: Hartsop Hall is a working farm, originally built in the sixteenth-century, though it has been extensively rebuilt and altered since. It was once the home of the de Lancasters, later of Sir John Lowther, who became the first Viscount Lonsdale, at the end of the seventeenth-century.

In the eighteenth-century, the Hall was extended across an ancient right of way, with the result that the right of way ran through the house. It is said that at least one dalesman used to make a point, from time to time, of ceremoniously walking the right of way.

Brothers Water: Once known as Broad Water, this attractive spread of water was renamed after two brothers, said to have drowned there.

Syke Side Farm: Much of the land around Syke Side Farm buildings is given to caravanners and campers. But the farm for forty years was the home of 'Old Charlie Dixon', who died there in 1936 at the age of eighty three. Charlie never left the Lake District, but he became world famous, for he was the original shepherd in some of the most famous pastoral photographs ever taken - 'The Shepherd and the Lost Sheep', 'A Westmorland Shepherd', and many more, lost to modern generations, but revered by those photographers for whom the Box Brownie was a State of the Art device.

Sheep

The sheep most commonly associated with the Lake District are the Herdwicks, a hardy breed, capable of withstanding the often fierce Lakeland winters. In the dales of the central and eastern fells, it is not uncommon, however, to find Swaledales replacing the traditional Herdwicks, or cross-breeding with them. Swaledales are almost as hardy as the Herdwicks, but tend to produce more lambs. They have a distinctive black face with a white muzzle, and their horns are often used to make ornate carved crooks.

WALK 2:

Dovedale, Dove Crag and Caiston Beck

Likened by one eighteenth-century writer to a "soft and delicate maiden", Dovedale is one of the most attractive dales in Lakeland, yet by comparison, it is relatively infrequently-visited. Soft and delicate might be one view of Dovedale, but wild and magnificent would do just as nicely. The crags that abound in Dovedale, and its near neigh-bour Deepdale, are renowned among the rock climbing fra-ternity for their severity and quality. Walkers simply pass them by, but not without a sense of occasion. Ironically, few walkers bother to pass by since Dove Crag, the objec-tive of this walk, is generally not considered to be worthy of such singular attention, and is normally included in a tiresome trail around the Fairfield Horseshoe. Thankfully, closer acquaintance shows how first impressions can be so misleading, for Dove Crag, approached through Dovedale, and left by way of Caiston Glen, ranks among the finest rounds in Lakeland.

For children, this will represent the first real opportunity to get to grips with a major fell, and involves some fairly energetic exercise. Although the route is largely easy to follow, walls and fences being excellent guides in the upper reaches, it is not a walk to tackle in poor visibility. Stout walking boots for everyone are essential.

> **Start:** Cow Bridge car park. GR 403134
> **Total Distance:** 12km (7½ miles)
> **Height gain:** 665m (2180 feet)
> **Difficulty:** Strenuous, and in-volves considerable height gain. Some previous experience of rough fell-walking at lower levels is essential. This is a good walk on which to start aiming for the heights.

THE WALK:

From the car park set off across the nearby bridge, spanning Goldrill Beck, and turn left through a gate on to a broad track running alongside, and later slightly above, the beck. This start is the same as that for the preceding walk around Brothers Water, but the two walks part company at Hartsop Hall Farm. Once you have

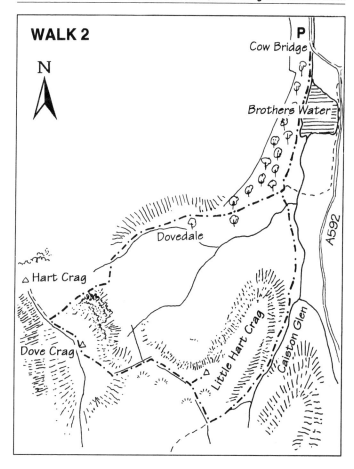

WALK 2

N

Cow Bridge

P

Brothers Water

Dovedale

△ Hart Crag

Dove Crag

Little Hart Crag

Caiston Glen

A592

reached Hartsop Hall, stay on the track going right. You soon meet a signposted path heading left for Kirkstone Pass and Scandale - this is the route by which you will return. Meanwhile, keep right at this point (signposted: Dove Crag) to begin what is a truly delightful ascent.

As with the woodlands through which you have just walked, there is an abundance of birdlife in the woodlands that lead into Dovedale, enlivening the walk with their song and displays. Jessica Lofthouse, writing in the late-1940s said, of Dovedale: "...a sweet little dale, a green

15

cradle among crags, sprinkled with hazel woods and berried rowans, with the beck, crystal-clear, chuckling over bright stones."

Follow the path, as it climbs steadily higher across the valley wall to gain a kind of sanctuary beneath the stern cliffs of Dove Crag.

This is a remarkable setting, as wild and rugged as any you will find in Lakeland, and by itself worthy of your attention. Which leads to the point that if anyone is feeling less than 100%, the best idea is to retrace your steps, and save what follows for another day.

To the right of the cliff a gully of scree, grass and projecting rock ribs is the onward route.

The gully is quite often running with water, too, and children should be restrained from getting too far ahead.

Take care as you ascend, finally to reach a high, wide hollow, with Dove Crag on your left, and Hart Crag on your right. This is Houndshope Cove, in which a small tarn often reposes.

Climb up out of Houndshope Cove on a continuing path to reach a line of cairns that leads to a wall across the saddle between Dove Crag and Hart Crag.

Here, turn left, following the wall for a few hundred yards to the top of Dove Crag.

Save for a large cairn, the top of Dove Crag is rather undistinguished, but the panoramic view makes the effort of climbing this high well worthwhile: only to the northwest is the view obstructed, by the mass of Fairfield, the highest summit in what can now be seen to be a fine horseshoe of fells.

THE WAY BACK:

To return to Brothers Water, continue south along the ridge, following the wall, until you meet a fenceline. Turn left here (east), and follow the fence down towards a neat summit, Little Hart Crag.

When I recently revisited this walk it was to find rusted strands of old fence wire still half-buried in the grass, as they have been for years. They can trip the unwary, and great care should be exercised against this hazard until you are well beyond Little Hart Crag.

As you descend along the fenceline from Dove Crag, you encounter first a steep section, and, as the gradient eases, a fence going off to the left - ignore this, and stay with the on-going fence, still running roughly northeastwards. A short way on, the fence veers right (southeast) as it moves on to the knolly top of Little Hart Crag. When it changes direction again, even more to the south, leave the fence for a while to walk to the top of Little Hart Crag, in a short dose of blatant peak-bagging.

Return to the fence and follow it down to meet a wall. A brief left and right along the wall, then sets you heading down beside the wall to reach a stile at the head of Scandale Pass.

Go left here and follow the path down into Caiston Glen.

Caiston Glen is a charming retreat that is not often visited, possessing a splendid display of miniature cascades. Lower down it joins forces with Kirkstone Beck, before flowing on into Brothers Water.

Follow the path all the way down the glen, passing, just before you cross Dovedale Beck, the site of an ancient settlement.

Press on, over the beck and through a cluster of gates to reach your outward route close by Hartsop Hall. Retrace your steps from here. Or, if still feeling energetic, complete the circuit of Walk 1 around Brothers Water, it won't add much to the overall distance.

OPTIONAL EXTRA:

When you reach the saddle between Dove Crag and Hart Crag, you can divert, right, up beside the wall to visit the top of Hart Crag. Return the same way. This will add one kilometre (½ mile), and 75m (245 feet) of ascent, but will give you a fine view of the continuing ridge to Fairfield - a fine prospect, but one which, from this walk, may prove one fell too far.

Dove Crag

Before the Second World War rock climbers tended away from the crags of the eastern fells, preferring, as they saw it, better fare elsewhere. Dove Crag was an exception. In 1910 'Rusty' Westmorland, pioneered routes on the crag, though little further exploration took place until 1939, when an aptly named climb, *Hangover*, was devised up the leaning central buttress. Gradually, the reputation of Dove Crag expanded, and before long was attracting the attention of all the great climbers of the 1950s and 1960s.

High on its face is a cave, known as a Priest Hole. Unseen from below, but with a commanding view, it was probably quarried by Dalesman, and has seen frequent service as a bivouac.

WALK 3:
Hayeswater

Set in a grassy hollow, carved during the Ice Age, and fashioned by the winds of time since then, Hayeswater would not rank highly on a list of the most attractive tarns in Lakeland, and few walkers

Start: Car park, Hartsop village.
GR 410131
Total Distance: 4km (2½ miles)
Height gain: 245m (805 feet)
Difficulty: Easy; a steady uphill stroll

bother to go there unless bound for higher things. Yet it lies in a perfectly shaped glacial corrie, with abundant evidence of moraine deposits all around, and, on a warm summer's day, away from the main pathway near its outflow, it offers a splendid high mountain setting, usually sheltered from the wind, in which to enjoy a picnic.

The approach walk is at a steady gradient, and passes through pleasant scenery, with an outstanding view into the side valley of Pasture Bottom to Threshthwaite Mouth, a high mountain pass linking this corner of Patterdale with the next valley, Troutbeck.

THE WALK:

The car park lies at the end of the road through Hartsop village. Leave it by a gate and follow a metalled roadway. Later, just after another gate, take a right fork leading to a bridge over Hayeswater Gill.

The great grassy fell in front of you is Gray Crag, a tiring, trackless and demanding way on to the tops. To its right lies the long and pleasant valley of Pasture Bottom, and on its right, the craggy flanks of Hartsop Dodd,

that lead on past the dark buttress of Raven Crag, above which lies the rocky summit of Stony Cove Pike, also known as Caudale Moor and John Bell's Banner, in the last case, thought to be named after a seventeenth-century curate of Ambleside, whose parochial boundary, or 'banner', ran across the top of this fell - a spiritual threshhold, perhaps?

Once across Hayeswater Gill, the onward path takes you to another gate in the intake wall,

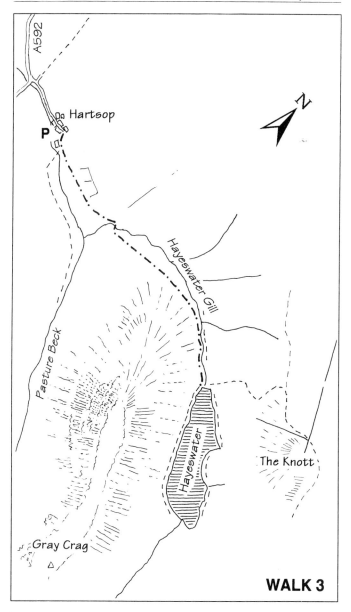

WALK 3

before continuing easily up to the outflow of Hayeswater.

The tarn, almost exactly a kilometre in length (just over half a mile), is cradled in a vast grassy bowl. Along its western shoreline, beneath the steep slopes of Gray Crag there are some excellent examples of glacial moraine, large hummocky mounds formed at the end of the last Ice Age, about 10,000 years ago, as the glacier that filled and sculpted this hollow retreated and dumped its debris along its margin, rather as an ebbing tide deposits along the tide mark.

A walk around the tarn, making use of sheep tracks and an incomplete path, is quite feasible, though it is wet and boggy where streams flow in, and around the inflow of Hayeswater Gill.

Directly above the tarn, to the east, rises The Knott, a neat circular summit with a commanding view (see Optional Extra).

THE WAY BACK:

The return journey simply retraces your steps.

OPTIONAL EXTRA:

Calling for a much greater expenditure of energy, but presenting no other difficulties, the summit of The Knott may be reached by a steep grassy path that can be seen climbing the fellside beyond the Hayeswater dam. In its upper reaches the path zigzags a little to ease the gradient before passing through a collapsed wall above which lies the summit.

From this new vantage point, there is a good view across a narrow neck of land, the Straits of Riggindale, to High Street, the highest fell in this group of hills.

This optional extra will add another two kilometres (1¼ miles) of total walking distance, and 315m (1035feet) of height gain, so be sure you want to take it on before you set off.

Return by the same route.

ALONG THE WAY:

Hartsop: The tiny community of Hartsop is, as Molly Lefebure describes in *Cumbrian Discovery*, "quaint in the truest sense of that much abused word". It retains many features to tell of its former self-sufficiency - a corn-drying kiln, spinning galleries, and traces of lead mining, near the confluence of Pasture Beck and Hayeswater Gill.

Spinning galleries are a familiar characteristic of Lakeland farm architecture. These wooden galleries, quite a few of which are still open to view, were formed by carrying the roof beyond the wall, the resultant space underneath the extended eaves forming useful storage space.

WALK 4:
Angletarn Pikes and Angle Tarn

This popular walk is a good way of finding out how young legs take to an uphill path, without going to extremes. The climb to Boardale Hause is a steady pull made light by the ever-swelling view across

Start: Patterdale car park. GR 396159
Total Distance: 8km (5 miles)
Height gain: 429m (1380 feet)
Difficulty: Moderate; a long steady uphill walk. Potentially confusing in mist.

the valley to the high fells west of Patterdale - St Sunday Crag, Fairfield, Dollywaggon Pike and Helvellyn - while the on-going path, with only nominal climbing to do, works a way in and out of rounded hummocks before clambering to the rocky topknot of Angletarn Pikes. A splendid picnic site, on a fine day, awaits only a short distance further, at Angle Tarn.

Although the walk is linear, leaving you to come back by the same route, there is the possibility of extending it to visit Hayeswater and Hartsop village, and to take in the handiwork of Goldrill Beck, where post-glacial alluvial deposits have significantly shortened the former length of Ullswater.

THE WALK:

Leave the car park and turn right, along the road for a short distance, until you reach the George Starkey Memorial Hut on the right. Immediately beside the building (anything but a hut!) take a broad track leading to Side Farm.

En route you cross Goldrill Beck, largely responsible thousands of years ago for the formation of much of the flat ground at the southern end of the dale.

Continue between the build-ings at Side Farm, and turn right on a broad track (signposted: Angle Tarn and Boredale Hause), heading for the cluster of buildings at Rooking.

At a gate, turn left, through another gate, to reach the open fellside, following the path up and right, with the onward route now plainly visible across the slopes ahead. At a fork, keep to the higher path.

Both paths lead to the same place, but the higher path also

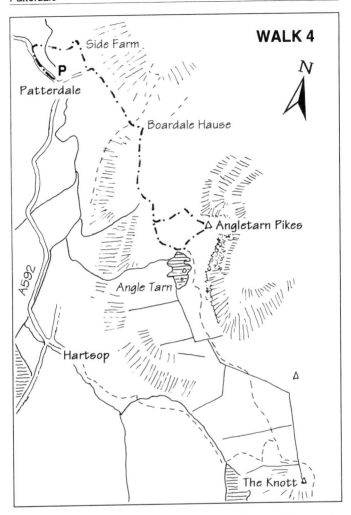

WALK 4

N

Side Farm

P

Patterdale

Boardale Hause

Δ Angletarn Pikes

A592

Angle Tarn

Hartsop

Δ

The Knott Δ

leads to a convenient bench from which to take in the ever-increasing panorama of fells across the valley.

The path continues uneventfully to Boardale Hause, a flat, grassy col between the hillocks that run on towards Angletarn Pikes and the bulk of Place Fell to the north.

As you reach a couple of collapsed cairns, move right, to

cross a small beck, ignoring any paths going off to the left. Once across the beck, the on-going path is evident enough and pursues a pleasant course, twisting and turning in and out of hollows until the rocky tops of Angletarn Pikes come into view.

As they do, so a breathtaking view of Brothers Water and the Kirkstone Pass suddenly appears, through a gap in rocks.

The path continues past Angletarn Pikes, so leave it, near the foot of the Pikes, and climb to the northerly and higher top.

Descend to cross the brief boggy hollow that separates the Pikes, and climb to the southerly top, from where you gain a first glimpse of Angle Tarn below.

Head down towards the tarn, where you will rejoin the main path, left earlier. The tarn, a shapely stretch of water with tiny islands, is in a beautiful setting, and a fine spot to rest and enjoy lunch.

THE WAY BACK:

The most direct is to retrace your steps, no less pleasant a prospect for going back the way you came.

As you do you will feel as though you are walking directly into that magnificent spread of mountains to the west - St Sunday Crag, Dollywaggon Pike, Nethermost Pike and Helvellyn, with the popular rocky scramble

of Striding Edge prominent in the foreground.

OPTIONAL EXTRA:

From Angle Tarn it is possible to extend this walk by a path that ultimately heads for a minor summit, The Knott.

Follow the path around Angle Tarn, and climb easily with improving views, to a level stretch of ground near Satura Crag. Go through a gate and pass beneath Satura Crag, beyond which muddy ground and an undulating path, that crosses Prison Gill and Sulphury Gill, leads to a meeting with a path ascending from Hayeswater, far below.

When you meet this ascending path (or earlier if conditions underfoot are dry) descend to the outflow of Hayeswater, and follow the path out of the valley.

Keep on, through the village, until just before reaching the main valley road (A592), you can turn right on a minor access road, later a track, that pursues a delightful route along the base of the fells you have just crossed, past Dubhow, Beckstones and Crookabeck, until, on reaching Rooking, you can follow a minor road, left, back to Patterdale, meeting the road only a short distance away from the car park.

This extension will take the total walking distance to 12½ km (8 miles), but will not significantly add to the height gain.

WALK 5:
Place Fell

Place Fell totally dominates Patterdale and Glenridding, so much so that it is virtually impossible for any red-blooded hill walker to ignore it for long, nor should they. The face overlooking Ullswater is unremittingly steep, cloaked in heather, bracken and juniper, and gives the impression of a fairly uncomplicated summit, with fine symmetrical lines. Yet Place Fell is an outstanding height on which to spend a day; its complex summit a superb panoramic viewpoint in spite of the fell's modest elevation.

> **Start:** Patterdale car park. GR 396159
> **Total Distance:** 6 km (4 miles)
> **Height gain:** 510 m (1675 feet)
> **Difficulty:** Moderate: a sustained ascent, with little respite, except at Boardale Hause. Since the object of the exercise is the view, save Place Fell for a fine day.

The possibility exists to tackle Place Fell from the north, from Sandwick: the following walk, however, has its ambitions firmly rooted in Patterdale, and is the shortest of the available routes. It was on Place Fell, as I chatted with a father and his seven year old son, plodding happily up from Boardale Hause, that the seeds from which 'Walks with Children' later flourished were first sown.

THE WALK:

The first part of this walk coincides with that for the ascent of Angletarn Pikes (Walk 4), as far as Boardale Hause.

Leave the car park and turn right, along the road, until you reach the George Starkey Memorial Hut. There, take a broad track leading to Side Farm, crossing Goldrill Beck en route.

Go between the farm buildings, and turn right on a broad track (signposted: Angle Tarn and Boredale Hause). Follow this track to a gate at Rooking, where you can turn left and immediately through another gate to gain the open fellside. Take to the ensuing path that climbs a little and then slants, right, across the side of Place Fell, rising all the way to Boardale Hause.

Place Fell lies due north from the Hause, across which a proliferation of paths can be confus-

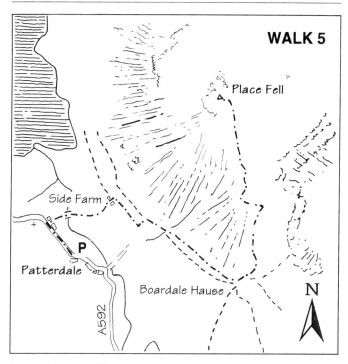

WALK 5

Place Fell

Side Farm

P

Patterdale

Boardale Hause

A592

N

ing in misty conditions. In poor visibility it is all too easy to wander off on the wrong track from Boardale Hause.

With the objective, Place Fell, firmly in view, take a path rising gently to the left from the Hause. It soon forks; when it does keep left, gradually swinging to a more northerly direction, heading for the lower slopes of Place Fell, up which a clear path can now be seen to rise. *[The path to the right at the fork leads over into Boardale, the object of Walk 6.]*

By steady persistence, and with frequent pauses to regain your breath, gradually you make an impression on what seems like a formidable slope - it isn't, in reality. A wide zigzag eases the gradient when it needs it most, but don't be misled into thinking the first large cairn looming overhead is the summit. This is but a minor outlier, Round How: Place Fell summit lies a short way further on, surmounted by a cairn and an Ordnance Survey trig pillar.

There are many comfortable niches among the rocky outcrops on the top of Place Fell from which to take in the panorama, and attempt to identify the surrounding and distant fells. The heights of Helvellyn and Fairfield are most outstanding, their summits standing high above glacially-carved corries. Further north you can see the splendid southern flank of Blencathra, with an uninspiring profile of Skiddaw beyond. On a clear day, you get a glimpse of the Solway Firth, and the land of Dumfries and Galloway in southern Scotland.

THE WAY BACK:

The best way back is the way you came, a journey, the pleasure of which is not in any way diminished by retracing your steps.

Ullswater

Ullswater has always been regarded as one of the most outstandingly beautiful expanses of water in Lakeland; its distinctive form creating new vistas with every bend in the road.

The lake is the second largest in the Lake District, and if its twisted shape were straightened, it would extend almost eight miles from Pooley Bridge to Patterdale. Were it not for the action of Goldrill Beck, and the many side streams that feed into it, collectively depositing mountain debris and silt, Ullswater would no doubt extend further towards the head of the dale, beyond Brothers Water, to the foot of the Kirkstone Pass.

That the lake was formed by glacial action is beyond question; it displays many of the features typical of glaciation, and in places exceeds 200ft in depth.

The name, Ullswater, derives from Baron Lyulph. Lyulph's Tower, along the northern shore of the lake is an eighteenth-century folly constructed by one of the dukes of Norfolk. It stands on or near the site of a fortress belonging to Lyulph, the first Baron Greystoke. 'Lyulph' stems from Ulf, or L'Ulf, the Scandinavian for wolf, hence Ulf's Water.

Celia Fiennes, on her 'Great Journey to Newcastle and to Cornwall' in 1698, commented of Ullswater: "its full of such sort of stones and slatts in the bottom as the other [Windermere], neer the brimm where its shallowe you see it cleer to the bottom; this is secured on each side by such formidable heights."

WALK 6:
Boardale

'Boardale' or 'Boredale'? Quite when the former became the latter is not certain. Modern maps don't help; some give one rendition, some the other. Baddeley's guide to 'The Lake District', one of the earliest detailed guidebooks to appear, calls it Boardale, and wild boars certainly roamed the wooded slopes of this part of Britain until not all that long ago. Quite why these things change seldom becomes clear, but for the late Alfred Wainwright, doyen of Lakeland fell guidebooks, it was Boardale, so that is how it will remain.

Start: Patterdale car park. GR 396159
Total Distance: 13km (8 miles)
Height gain: 300m (985 feet)
Difficulty: Moderate: a sustained ascent to Boardale Hause, leads to a brief rocky descent into Boardale. The shore path, used on the return, has a great many undulations, which can prove tiring towards the end of the walk.

The walk that follows makes use of quite a stretch of the valley roadway, entering the dale from its head, from where it appears with remarkable suddenness and breathtaking beauty. By comparison with Lakeland's many other valleys, Boardale is virtually unknown, so the traffic you meet when you reach the road is light. Even so, young children and dogs will need controlling between Boardalehead Farm and Sandwick Bay. The return along the shores of Ullswater is one of the finest low-level walks in Lakeland.

THE WALK:

From the car park turn left into Patterdale village, and soon, at a bend, take a minor road leading left over Goldrill Bridge to the cluster of cottages at Rooking. Follow the road up to a gate, turning right through it to gain the open fellside. Take the ris-ing path slanting right, across the fellside, to Boardale Hause. This is the same path used by the two previous walks, approached from a different direction.

As you reach the Hause, go left on a gently rising path. This soon forks, with the left branch heading for Place Fell, and the right branch, the way you should go, continuing more or less ahead to reach an unsuspected and quite dramatic rocky gully at the head of Boardale.

Near the top of the gully, inspection chambers mark the line of the Hayeswater Viaduct, while lower down there is clear evidence of mine working.

Taking care on the loose rocks that fill the gully, descend to reach a more substantial path easing down into the valley.

The long rocky ridge on your right is Beda Fell, while far ahead, at the end of the valley, rises shapely Hallin Fell.

All you need do now is to follow the path down into the valley. At Boardale Head Farm, bypassed by a permissive path on the left if the farmyard is busy, you meet the valley road, a quiet and attractive route that accompanies Boardale Beck, and later crosses it at a fine spot for lunch, or a short break.

Continue following the road until you can take a branch to the left leading down to Sandwick. Ignore another minor road on the right, near Doe Green Farm, and press on around the grassy spur of Sleet Fell as far as a signpost on the left, indicating the way back to Patterdale.

Go left here, leaving the road, and following a clear path above a wall. After crossing Scalehow Beck by a footbridge, the path heads for the lakeshore of Ullswater, glimpses of which have already come and gone as you followed the path.

Now what follows is sheer delight: a twisting, turning, rising, falling pathway, never in doubt, and seeming to go on forever, leads first into woodland, and out again at Silver Bay, another perfect spot for a break.

Across the lake, lie the recesses of Glencoynedale, the dark heights of Sheffield Pike, and Glenridding, from where steamers sail up and down the lake during the summer months.

As you round Silver Point, so the path begins its undulations in earnest, flowing on in a series of dips and cols, each cause for a moment's rest, each drawing you on along the lake, until, finally you reach the end of the lake. The path widens to a farm access track, and descends to approach Side Farm.

On reaching the farm, **either** (1) go ahead for a short distance to a gate, continuing ahead beyond it on the minor road used on the outward route, **or** (2) turn right, between the farm buildings and stables, to follow the access track out to the main valley road. At the road turn left, reaching the car park in a matter of minutes.

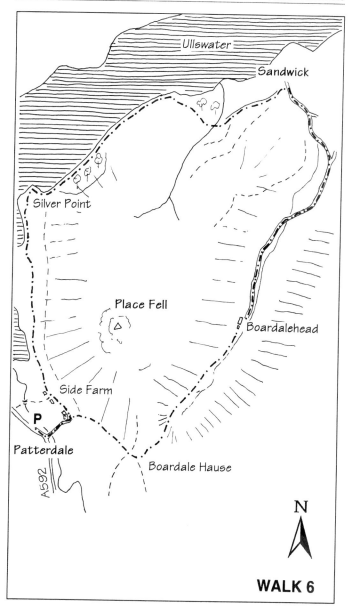

WALK 6

ALONG THE WAY:

Boardale Hause: *Boardale Hause is a long-established cross-valley route, a pony track linking Patterdale and Howtown.*

Foundations remaining on Boardale Hause are thought to be those of a thirteenth-century church, serving not only Patterdale, but the neighbouring valleys that collectively are known as Martindale. It would have been incredibly small, and became known as the Chapel-in-the-Hause. One suggestion, that it was built there during times of religious persecution, seems to overlook the prominence of the Hause as a through route.

Echoes from the Past

Lancelot Pattinson, from an established Patterdale family, lived a normal life in the dale until his wife died. Faced now with a family to raise, 'Lanty Patty', as he came to be known, moved his family into a cave near Goldrill Bridge, which later was named 'Lanty's Castle'. From this humble abode, Lanty managed to raise his family, and lived to be ninety-five himself, dying in 1865.

The Dukes of Norfolk, however, found a different way of amusing themselves, and kept a boat on the lake from which they would fire cannons to test the echoes across the lake. Thomas Rose commented: "The firing of a cannon causes an awful uproar, as if the foundations of every rock on the lake were giving way." He went on, suggesting that an orchestra might also have been present at some time: "a few wind instruments produce an entirely different effect: the most ravishing sounds fill the air, and form a thousand symphonies playing together from every part."

WALK 7:
Silver Bay

This brief walk along the shores of Ullswater is one of the most dramatically beautiful walks in the Lake District, combining the attractions of the lake, with its 'steamer' and sailing boats, and those of Nature itself - the craggy fells and deep, penetrating valleys across the lake, and the most pleasant walking through woodland on the lower slopes of Place Fell.

Start: Patterdale car park. GR 396159
Total Distance: 6km (3¾ miles)
Height gain: 100m (330 feet)
Difficulty: Easy: a delightful walk.

The return stage of the walk has many undulations, but each 'rise' brings a new vista, maintaining interest throughout, while the lake is a constant companion, on a still day reflecting the surrounding hills to perfection. At other times, as Molly Lefebure comments in Cumbrian Discovery: *"The lake surface becomes kaleidoscopic; now crossed with long, gleaming ripples, now dazzling with motes of sun-reflections as if suddenly garbed in a suit of lights, now in reaches solid as pewter, now slapping in small waves against huge, smooth old rocks from which trees grow at unbelievable angles."*

THE WALK:

Leave the car park and go left along the road to a bend, there taking a minor road over Goldrill Bridge to the cottages at Rooking. Keep on to the fell gate, and once through it (as if heading for Angle Tarn) climb a little and then take a path going left. The path heads northwards, always some distance above the lower path by which you will return.

With the most splendid scenery all around, the path presses on, aiming to the right of the conspicuous rocky top of Silver Crag. Eventually you reach a grassy saddle, to the east of Silver Crag, and at the top of a rocky ravine.

Here you gain your first view of Silver Bay, while looking back you see the whole valley spread out, rising to the Kirkstone Pass.

With care, descend the ravine to reach the grassy banks above Silver Bay.

The Bay is a most perfect spot for lunch, as is the nearby promontory of Silver Point, and many a lazy hour can be spent here.

THE WAY BACK:

To return, follow the pathway left, around Silver Crag, and stay on its up-and-down course, in and out of small copses, around rocky ribs, until finally you return to the civilisation of Side Farm.

The path is never in doubt, and provides numerous opportunities to digress and relax.

On reaching Side Farm **either** (1) go ahead for a short distance to a gate, continuing beyond it on the minor road used on the outward route, **or** (2) turn right, between the farm buildings and stables, to follow the access track out to the main valley road. At the road turn left, reaching the car park in a matter of minutes.

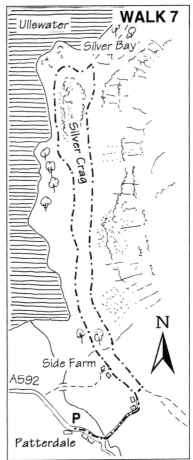

ALONG THE WAY:

Sheep: *Two types of sheep are farmed in Patterdale, the Herdwick and the Swaledale. During this walk you may well see both.*

Herdwicks are small and stocky, with white faces and legs. Their wool is coarse and grey, and only rams have spiral horns.

Lambs have black faces and legs.

Swaledales have black and white faces, with speckled legs. Their wool is closer and less grey. Both males and females have horns, though the rams have the better, more spiralled, display.

WALK 8:
Grisedale

This is a most pleasing walk in one of Lakeland's finest valleys, and follows the course of Grisedale Beck, itself flowing from Grisedale Tarn (see Walk 9). The walk is sufficiently varied to maintain interest throughout. There are numerous spots along the way at which to stop for a picnic, but avoid approaching the steep-sided and dangerous ravines (well off the path) through which Grisedale Beck flows in its upper reaches.

Start: Patterdale car park. GR 396159
Total Distance: 9½km (6 miles)
Height gain: 170m (555 feet)
Difficulty: Moderate: a pleasant walk on metalled roads or good paths. The first (and last) part is on a quiet farm access road, while the loop around the upper reaches of Grisedale is stony and uneven underfoot, with some undulation

The scenery is outstandingly beautiful at all times of the year, but in autumn especially the changing colours of the trees, the mix of deciduous and non-deciduous, the bracken and heather-clad hillsides, all bring colours which are not present at other times of the year. This is nowhere in Lakeland better exemplified than on this fine circuit of Grisedale.

THE WALK:

From the car park walk, right, along the road past Patterdale Church, following the road round until at a sharp right bend you can leave it for a narrow road that leads into Grisedale. Along the first part of the road there is a drystone wall on the left, and a wire fence on the right, topped by a strand of barbed wire. Continue past the entrance to Patterdale Hall Estate.

A short way along the road on the left you may notice a massive towering red-barked tree. This is a Western Red Cedar, otherwise known as the Giant Arbor-vitae. These are grown in Europe for timber, shelter, and in gardens, and often grow to a height in excess of 40m (135ft).

Follow the road as it bends right and begins a short uphill section that ends just after a cottage on the right.

33

Here, you find yourself above a small copse at the bottom of which flows Grisedale Beck. This small area of woodland is a particularly favoured haunt of great spotted woodpeckers, while the beck itself is frequented by dippers and members of the wagtail family.

Gradually the woodland copse is left behind and the right hand side of the path, still with a wire and barbed wire fence, opens up as the ground drops down to Grisedale Beck in one of its most lovely reaches.

Away to the right you can see the long path climbing across the hillside to a spot known as the "Hole in the Wall" which marks the start of Striding Edge, one of the most popular ways up Helvellyn. The high fell on your left is known as Birks, and leads up to an even higher mountain called St Sunday Crag, of which you will see more later.

There is a high drystone wall on the left here, and in a short while when the road bends sharply right, continue ahead through a gate (signposted: Grasmere: Grisedale Tarn). You remain on a metalled road surface for a while longer, but now there is open ground on the right, although the drystone wall still continues on the left.

*Very shortly the summit of St Sunday Crag comes into view, while directly ahead rises a mas-*sive ring of mountains which make up the southern end of the Helvellyn range.

Continue through another gate marking the entrance to Braesteads Farm - a small stepstile on the right. When the track branches off to the farm, continue ahead on what is now a stony track, keeping a drystone wall on the left and open meadows on the right.

Very soon the path comes close to the banks of Grisedale Beck, and here starts to undulate a little, becoming more stony and uneven underfoot. Continue to another gate and then beyond move away from the wall that has accompanied us so far as you approach Elmhow Farm. As you reach Elmhow a better view opens up of the steep upper slopes of St Sunday Crag.

Pass to the right of the farm buildings through a gate, and look down and to the right over Grisedale Beck to see an interesting stone-arched bridge built in traditional Lakeland style. At the next gate, with a barn directly ahead, the view of the crags of Nethermost Pike and Dollywagon Pike is especially impressive.

Keep to the left of the barn (signposted: Grisedale Tarn: Grasmere), and at a gate pass through the intake wall. St Sunday Crag now looms on the left, while ahead you can see a small

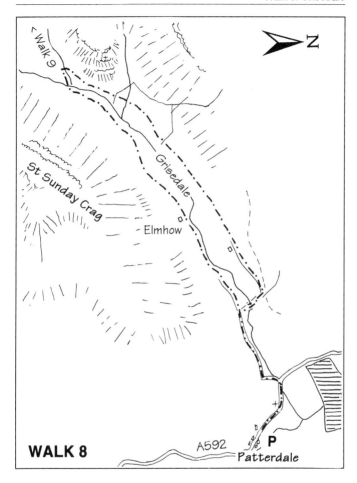

WALK 8

wooded copse. The path continues as a stony track - quite broad, and still undulating - but now with a wall on the right hand side.

On the opposite side of the valley, by which way you will return, you can see what must be one of the most impressive drystone walls in the Lake District, snaking its way up and across the hillside. The broken crags above the wall culminate in Striding Edge directly above and in due course lead on to Helvellyn.

As you round a bend, directly

ahead you see Nethermost Beck, spilling down the hillside between Striding Edge on the right, and Eagle Crag on the left. The beck issues from a hidden tarn directly above.

When the view ahead opens up you can see your onward path, which descends for a short while and then meanders upwards again. Past a small hillock on the left, in the far distance Ruthwaite Lodge comes into view, on the fellside below Dollywaggon Pike.

A short way further on the path starts to climb a little more energetically, becoming loose and stony underfoot, and young children might need a helping hand here for a while. As the path ascends, a slope appears on the right but the path remains broad and the slope, if you don't stray on to it, poses no real problem. The stony ascent is short-lived and levels out high above Grisedale Beck which, throughout the walk, is a delightful companion.

Suddenly, as you round a bend, the skyline ahead dips to the broad col that houses Grisedale Tarn. As you climb higher, so Grisedale Beck is channelled through a narrow gorge flanked with alder and silver birch. If you look across the other side of the ravine at this point you will see a broad path descending on the other side of the valley, and this is the way you will be going down. Directly above are the large craggy buttresses of Eagle Crag and Nethermost Pike.

After a short and fairly level stretch the path crosses a side stream by a wooden footbridge with a handrail, and begins the steady climb on a rough path strewn with small rocks to Ruthwaite Lodge.

All around at this point there are numerous glacial moraines, and up above on the right beneath Nethermost Pike, lies the hanging valley of Ruthwaite Cove.

Shortly now you reach another footbridge on the right. Cross this footbridge, to begin the return journey on the other side of the valley.

[Walkers intending to continue to Grisedale Tarn, should now refer to Walk 9.]

THE WAY BACK:

Once across the bridge, take the broad track on the true left bank of the beck.

As you descend this path there is an opportunity to look into the narrow ravine through which Grisedale Beck flows, in which you can see a number of small and attractive waterfalls not visible from the ascending path.

Gradually the path descends to the long intake wall you saw previously, the one that ascends right up the side of Striding Edge, and you pass through the wall at a kissing gate just a short way further on.

On the right stand the remains of an old barn or shepherd's hut. The path along this section is generally easier underfoot than it is on the opposite side.

The path continues, undulating around more glacial moraine, and comes to an iron gate in a fence just opposite a small hillock, wooded with Scots pine.

As you start to reach the cultivated part of the valley you encounter the enclosured fields once more, where the land is markedly improved compared with that outside the enclosure.

In places the return path is rocky but never difficult, at other times it is a smooth grassy track. Good progress is made as the path eases along above the intake wall. Unfortunately, there is a little sting in the tail, for as the path passes Blaebeck Farm it starts to climb, but only for a short while, and leads to an iron gate in a fence. Just a short way further on it levels off again and continues until it meets a path descending from Striding Edge.

When you meet the Striding Edge path you drop to a walled corner. Ignore the gate directly ahead - this option will take you to Lanty's Tarn and Glenridding - but turn right through a second gate, and descend fairly steeply to the farm access track you can see below. As you reach the access road, go through a kissing gate and continue ahead along the road and, by a bridge, cross Grisedale Beck. A short ascent leads up to the road by which the outward walk was started. Turn left along this road, and retrace your steps to Patterdale.

ALONG THE WAY:
Drystone Wall Enclosures: The drystone walls were built during the 18th and 19th centuries under the provisions of the Enclosure Acts. Much depended, of course, on a ready supply of rocks with which to work - no problem in Grisedale, as you can see. Alas, many of these monuments to a dying craft are falling into disrepair, and great care should be taken by everyone not to cause further damage to them.

Eagle Crag: The name, Eagle Crag, is a link with the days when eagles flew freely across the Lakeland landscape. For a long time they disappeared, persecuted to extinction, but have started to re-establish themselves in recent years.

Ruthwaite Lodge: Ruthwaite Lodge was once a shepherd's hut, but is used these days by Ullswater Outdoor Centre, as a base for outdoor pursuits.

WALK 9:
Grisedale Tarn

This logical extension of Walk 8 that took you around Grisedale is a little more demanding, and climbs beyond Ruthwaite Lodge by a rocky path to one of the most attractively-set tarns in Lakeland.

Start: Patterdale car park. GR 396159
Distance: 13km (8 miles)
Height gain: 390m (1280ft)
Difficulty: Follows Walk 8 (Moderate) to just below Ruthwaite Lodge. A rough and rocky mile lies beyond the Lodge, but always on a good path. Care is needed, especially on the descent, if the rocks are wet.

Surrounded entirely by the slopes of high fells, notably those of Fairfield and Dollywaggon Pike, Grisedale Tarn lies in a vast hollow among the mountains, and is a perfect objective for a day's walk, and a most dramatic setting in which to enjoy lunch.

The scenery of Grisedale is outstanding, but as you climb higher so the detail of glaciated corries and hanging valleys becomes more evident, sculptures on a monumental scale.

THE WALK:

Follow Walk 8 as far as the bridge crossing Grisedale Beck, but continue instead to Ruthwaite Lodge, a short distance ahead and uphill. Beyond the Lodge the path, which is never in doubt, continues to Grisedale Tarn.

The going becomes more rugged, with a greater number of fallen boulders and scree to contend with, though they serve better as a means of enlivening the walk than they do as an obstacle to progress. As you climb into the upper valley, swapping the towering slopes of St Sunday Crag for the ruggedness of Dollywaggon Pike, High Crag and Nethermost Pike, so it becomes narrower, and a ravine appears on the left, containing the outflow from Grisedale Tarn. The pointed peak up on the left is Cofa Pike, a satellite of the much more bulky Fairfield behind it. Likewise, on the right, the shapely peak you see is an outlier of Dollywaggon Pike, and is split by the dark chasm of a deep vertical chimney.

Follow the path as it continues

its rough course, almost horizontally, for a quarter of a mile.

Below, the grassy slopes are dotted with boulders of all shapes and sizes that thousands of years ago would have fallen from the crags above, or been cast aside haphazardly by a retreating glacier.

Gradually, the path begins its final climb to the tarn. Once more the going is rough, but beyond the possibility of tripping, there are no real objective dangers to worry about. Take care as the path crosses a couple of narrow boulder fields until, by a large cairn, you can turn to enjoy the retrospective view down the valley. At a second cairn

the gradient eases noticeably as you cross the last rocky section before bursting upon the tarn.

If you look ahead and to the left at this point you will see a metal signpost set below the path and on top of a small rock outcrop. This marks the location of a slate slab set into the rock face bearing the words of Wordsworth's poem The Brothers' Parting, which commemorates the parting of Wordsworth and his brother John, Captain of the Earl of Abergavenny, in which he perished in 1805.

By now you have climbed high enough to get a return view of Ullswater, with the shapely cone of Silver Crag beyond.

A few more minutes brings you to the tarn, beside which a scattering of rocky outcrops provide suitable places to rest and enjoy lunch.

Southeast of the tarn a wide spread of scree and boulders rises to the summit of Fairfield; southwest, less daunting is the grassy dome of Seat Sandal, a minor fell, usually by-passed by walkers. North of the tarn a tiresome treadmill of a path works steadily upwards to Dollywaggon Pike, a fine vantage point if you ever get there, but a very tiring process. It is much more enjoyable relaxing by the tarn and

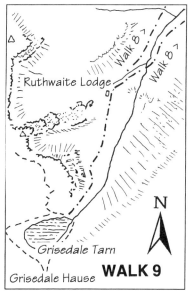

WALK 9

39

watching others struggle upwards!

Those of energetic disposition could follow a path all the way around the tarn, though it doesn't keep to the water's edge, and is eroded and boggy in a few places.

There is a tale that somewhere in Grisedale Tarn lies the crown of Duvenald, King of Strathclyde, who rejected his insignia of office, throwing it into the tarn, before taking to the pilgrim's staff.

THE WAY BACK:

When you are ready to return, simply retrace your steps as far as Ruthwaite Lodge. Beyond the Lodge you have a choice of routes: either go back down your outward route, or take the return route given in Walk 8.

ALONG THE WAY:

Ruthwaite Lodge: Built in 1854 as a shooting lodge, the building was more latterly used as a climbing hut by Sheffield University. Some time ago it was destroyed by fire, but has been restored and is now used by Outward Bound Ullswater. It was reopened on the 26 March 1993, and dedicated to the memory of Richard Reed and Mike Evans, tutors from Outward Bound Ullswater, who were killed while climbing Mount Cook in New Zealand in 1988.

John Wordsworth

"...two or three yards below the outlet of Grisedale Tarn, on a foot road by which a horse may pass to Patterdale..." Wordsworth and his brother John parted for the last time.

John was going to his ship, the *Earl of Abergavenny*, which tragically was wrecked on 5th February 1805 off Portland Bill.

Greatly moved by the loss of his brother, William returned to Grisedale Tarn, with his wife and sister in June, 1805, and later wrote the Elegiac Verses to his brother's memory.

Some accounts make of this incident, the final parting of the two brothers, more than is suggested by Dorothy's own *Journals*. In September 1802, Dorothy and William visited London, and during their stay met John, who was between East Indian voyages. That was the last time they saw him, for he never came north on his next return, in autumn 1804, and perished only a few months later. *The Brothers' Parting* probably refers to John's last visit to the Lake District.

WALK 10:
St Sunday Crag

One of the stated purposes of these books is to introduce children to the delights of walking in general, and hill walking in particular. Yet nothing will dampen enthusiasm more than constantly pursuing walks, however spectacular, that contain themselves in the valleys. Sooner or later, young eyes are going to be turned upwards, to the high fells. But it would be wrong to expose young children to the intricacies of, say, Striding Edge, without first making sure they have the energy and determination to complete the outing, and that they have no fear of heights.

Start: Patterdale car park. GR 396159
Total Distance: 9km (5½ miles)
Height gain: 695m (2280 feet)
Difficulty: Demanding, with considerable ascent, and sustained uphill walking. Some previous experience of rough fell walking at lower levels is essential.

The ascent of St Sunday Crag, which stands apart from both the Fairfield and Helvellyn ranges, has a tremendous feel of openness about it with magnificent views, and is a good 'test piece' for young legs, hearts and minds.

This is no easy ascent: it will demand a good deal of encouragement from parents, and should not be undertaken in less than perfect visibility and conditions. The rewards for perseverance are manifold, not least the satisfaction that comes from crossing the threshold from valley and mid-level walks to a high mountain ascent.

St Sunday Crag is a firm favourite with everyone who comes to know the Lakeland fells, and, for young children, its ascent is a commendable achievement.

THE WALK:

Although there is a shortcut from near the Patterdale Hotel, the walk begins by leaving the car park, right, along the road, heading for Patterdale Church. This will allow legs to be stretched, before starting the ascent.

Follow the road past the church, and take the next left, a

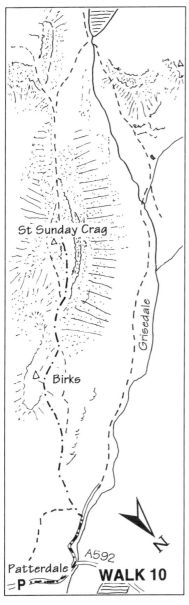

St Sunday Crag

Grisedale

Birks

A592

Patterdale

WALK 10

minor road, used on the walk into Grisedale (Walks 8 and 9). Stay with the road as it climbs easily, until, just after the last cottage on the right, you can leave the road for a path on the left (signposted), at a gate.

Go through the gate, and shortly bear right and follow a path, past a gate/stile, climbing steeply up the fellside. The path goes through light woodland before finally re-emerging on the open hillside. Continue to a stile over a wall, beyond which the path crosses the fellside before reaching a fork.

Directly before you is the minor summit, Birks, which can be omitted, by taking the right (and lower) branch, or included by climbing steeply up to the left. The top of Birks is grassy, and the highest point marked by a modest cairn.

Now, all that remains is to tackle the slopes of St Sunday Crag which lie before you.

Go down to the broad col below St Sunday Crag, where you rejoin the lower path, and from there climb the ridge directly ahead, steeply upwards. A path slanting leftwards from just above the col also reaches the summit plateau, by a slightly longer, but easier route. This used to be the main line of ascent, but has fallen from favour over the years.

The summit of St Sunday Crag stands towards the southern end of the plateau, marked by a large cairn.

The view, once you have recovered breath sufficiently to appreciate it, is outstanding. The fells of the Helvellyn massif rise to the northwest, but it is the closer proximity of Fairfield, Hart Crag and Dove Crag, that commands your attention more forcefully.

THE WAY BACK:

Return by retracing your steps, taking care on the two major steep sections.

When you have almost returned to the road, turn right, instead of going through the gate/stile, and follow a good path that trips across the northern end of Birks, to reach Patterdale close by the hotel and car park.

OPTIONAL EXTRA:

If the ascent proved less tiring than you thought, you can extend the walk, with no further height gain, but taking the total distance to 14km (8¾ miles). (NOTE: When you reach the top of St Sunday Crag you will have covered a little under three miles. This Optional Extra leaves you with 6 miles still to do, half of which, in spite of going downhill all the time, is still demanding, both of care and attention.)

Continue along the summit ridge of St Sunday Crag, descending on a clear path to reach a cairn on Deepdale Hause. The cairn marks the departure, right, of a slanting and narrow path leading down to Grisedale Tarn.

From the tarn, you now head into Grisedale, by turning right, after crossing the outflow of the tarn, to reach a broad, stony track descending to Ruthwaite Lodge. Below the Lodge, ignore a footbridge spanning the beck on your left, and continue to another footbridge, with a handrail, across Grisedale Beck. Beyond the bridge, the path eases downwards, eventually reaching easier going near Elmhow Farm.

From the farm, follow the access road, until you reach the metalled surface, which then leads you down to Grisedale Bridge and the main valley road. Turn right, and follow the road back past Patterdale Church to the car park.

WALK 11:
Lanty's Tarn and the Greenside Mine

Lead was first discovered at Greenside as early as 1650, but the mine did not come into operation until late in the eighteenth-century. The greatest period of mining activity was in the first half of the nineteenth-century, by which time Greenside was the largest lead mine in England. The principal ore mined was galena, or lead sulphide, which was then smelted to produce 80% lead: it also produced 350g of silver per ton.

Start: Glenridding car park. GR 386170
Total Distance: 6km (3¾ miles)
Height gain: 185m (605 feet)
Difficulty: Easy: a little uphill work at the start.

Mining operations at Greenside finally ceased in 1962, and many of the buildings removed, though some have been put to other uses. As with many mines, Greenside has its store of disasters, the most notable occurring on the 29th October 1927 when the dam in Keppel Cove burst its embankment sending a flood wave down the valley, causing damage to property and livestock on a wide scale, but, surprisingly taking no human life. In 1959 the mine was taken over by the Atomic Energy Commission for conducting seismic test explosions underground.

The walk that follows, as well as visiting the Greenside Mine, for a taste of industrial archaeology, also takes in Lanty's Tarn, a diminutive tarn in a delightful setting, and with a fine retrospective view of Ullswater.

THE WALK:

Leave the car park and head for the main road, turning right to cross Glenridding Bridge. Go immediately right on a narrow road, following the course of Glenridding Beck, past the Post Office and the Public Hall.

The road deteriorates to a stony track, and a short way further on forks. Go left (signposted: Lanty's Tarn. Helvellyn), and soon pass a line of cottages on your right, to reach a wooden footbridge. Cross the stream and start climbing steeply to a series of zigzags that ease the gradient.

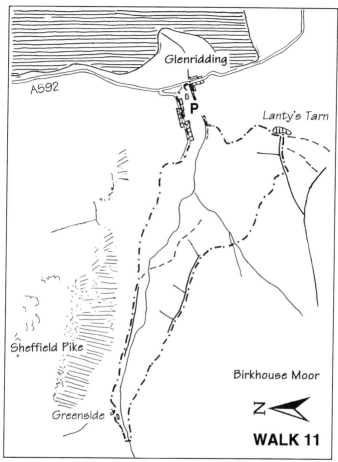

The acquired dodge of stopping to take a photograph when you most need a breather will here be amply justified, since the glimpses through the trees and over rooftops of Ullswater are very attractive, and worthy of frequent attention.

The onward route is never in doubt, and passes through a kissing gate before moving into a more open landscape.

The great mass of fell on your right is Birkhouse Moor, and to its right you can pick out the Greenside Mine complex set against the dark scree and rocks of Sheffield Pike.

45

Continuing upwards, ignore a gate in a wall, but press on until a brief descent brings you to another gate, with Lanty's Tarn beyond, set in a pleasant glade of pine and deciduous woodland.

[Just before the Lanty's Tarn gate, a short detour, left, will take you on to Keldas, a small summit with a massive view.]

Lanty's Tarn is a very relaxing spot, but is not renowned for peace and quiet, being too close to civilisation for that. It was built as a small reservoir, but is no less idyllic on that account.

Before the end of the tarn is reached a path ascends, right, following a wall. Follow this and once clear of the woodland cross the wall at a gate.

From the gate, go ahead, away from the wall, on an indistinct path, that soon improves as you approach a wall and head for Mires Beck.

Press on beyond the beck, still with a wall on your right, and eventually you cross a disused water leat before descending to reach an iron bridge spanning Red Tarn Beck.

Cross the bridge and go right to reach the mine buildings: some are used as an outdoor adventure centre, while the former stables now see service as a youth hostel.

The mine workings have largely been filled in and made safe, but enough remains to give the site an aura of hard and hazardous industry.

THE WAY BACK:

The return to Glenridding simply follows the descending broad track by which the mine buildings and youth hostel are approached. This track leads directly back to the village and the car park.

Mining in the Lake District

Mining in the Lake District is not exclusive to Greenside, of course: the remains of mining for copper, lead and other metals lie scattered over many Lakeland fells. Greenside, however, has the distinction of being the most consistently successul lead mine in the district, working continuously for 140 years, and it was remarkable, too, for adopting the best available technology in its operations.

More information about the Greenside mine, and others, is available from the Cumbria Amenity Trust Mining History Society, 46 St Luke's Street, Barrow-in-Furness, Cumbria.

WALK 12:
Sheffield Pike

Motorists driving alongside Ullswater may well know Sheffield Pike rather better than walkers. From the car it is the prominent, craggy lump just northwest of Glenridding, terminating in a lesser craggy lump, Glenridding Dodd.

Start: Glenridding car park. GR 386170.
Total Distance: 9km (5½ miles)
Height gain: 520m (1705 feet)
Difficulty: Moderate, in good conditions. Steep walking, in short doses. Not recommended in less than perfect conditions; the top of Sheffield Pike is very confusing in mist.

Patterdale, however, favours walkers bound for the heights of Fairfield, Helvellyn and the Dodds, and so it is that for every pair of booted feet that tread across Sheffield Pike's' lonely summit, there will be five hundred or more on Helvellyn.

Sheffield Pike is not a glamorous fell: it boasts no extended rocky ridges, no airy traverses, and no delightfully cascading becks - though Mossdale Beck to the east and Glencoyne Beck to the north have their moments. To add to this grim litany, the activities of the Greenside Mining Company have seen to it that much of the southern flank of the mountain is scarred irreparably.

Thankfully, Sheffield Pike, seemingly against all the odds, does have a more attractive profile, made use of on this walk.

THE WALK:
The first stage of the walk ambles along the lakeshore as far as Mossdale Bay.

Leave the car park at its northern end and walk out to the main road, crossing it in a short while to reach a Permissive Path along the water's edge. When you have crossed in-flowing Mossdale Beck, keep an eye open for a signposted track on the opposite side of the road, climbing into Glencoyne Wood alongside a wall.

The track climbs past a row of cottages that has the unusual name of Seldom Seen, a tiny cluster of buildings built long ago for miners at the Greenside Mine.

Beyond Seldom Seen the

track ends and a path continues to a gate near a wall junction. Go through the gate and keep right, along an adjoining wall. Follow this until it ends abruptly, and then follow a path rising, half left, across the steep slopes of Sheffield Pike above, to Nick Head, a conspicuous saddle between Sheffield Pike and the crags of Green Side and Glencoyne Head.

Turn left (east) at the saddle, and climb easily to the top of Sheffield Pike. The summit is a craggy affair, with many undulations, small tarns and boggy ground.

THE WAY BACK:

There are a number of possible ways back:-

(1) *The measured and preferred route*: Continue east across the top of Sheffield Pike, then moving southeast to a group of small tarns near a minor outlier, Heron Pike, its location marked by an iron boundary marker post. Drop down past Heron Pike and then turn left (northeast) to intersect a wall at the upper limit of Glencoyne Wood. Follow this wall northwards (left) until you reach the wall junction and gates met with on the ascent. Retrace your steps from there.

(2) *The easiest:* Return to the saddle, and there take a path descending southwest to reach the upper workings of the Greenside Mine. Follow the path down through the workings to the former mine buildings now used as a youth hostel and outdoor pursuits centre, and take the broad track running down into the Glenridding valley from there.

(3) *The shortest:* Go towards Heron Pike, as described above, and continue down the ensuing southeast ridge. You meet the same wall as before, but further to the south, at a corner. From here move away from the wall, and descend the dry bed of a shallow gully, that cuts across steep bracken-clad slopes: keep to the right of the prominent rocky bluff, Blaes Crag, and follow a path down to the Greenside Road. Turn left along the road, and walk out to the car park at Glenridding.

The National Trust

Much of the Lake District is a working landscape of busy farms. More than eighty of those farms are owned by the National Trust, along with large tracts of open countryside and buildings of special merit and historical significance.

The Trust is currently going to great lengths to improve and maintain its properties, and in particularl is repairing and renovating walls, farm buildings, and endeavouring to re-establish native British hardwoods, predominantly sessile oak

WALK 13:
Aira Force and Gowbarrow Fell

Aira Force is one of Lakeland's most attractive waterfalls, and is part of an estate purchased by the National Trust in 1913. The land immediately surrounding the Force has been landscaped as

Start: Aira Force car park. GR 401201
Total Distance: 7km (4½ miles)
Height gain: 320m (1050 feet)
Difficulty: Moderate: not recommended beyond Aira Force in poor visibility.

a Victorian park, complete with arboretum. Molly Lefebure observes: "Its chief beauty lies in the down-leaping motion of white water piercing the chasm of green tree-filled gloom...There is a kind of Romantic perfection about all this which is almost too good to be true."

Aira Force is the product of Aira Beck which gathers its water from the grounded, grassy summits of the Dodds, far in the recesses of Deepdale, and close by the summit of Stybarrow Dodd.

To the east lies Gowbarrow Park, rising to the modest height of Gowbarrow Fell, from the shores of Ullswater, along which William and Dorothy Wordsworth saw the daffodils immortalised in William's poem, which begins: "I wandered lonely as a cloud..."

The walk that follows first visits Aira Force before climbing to the top of Gowbarrow Fell: the scenery is outstanding throughout.

THE WALK:

Leave the car park at its northern end and follow a stony path until you can turn, right, through a swing gate. Continue to a wooden footbridge over Aira Beck.

After crossing the bridge the path on the far bank divides at the top of steps. Go left along the lower path, with Aira Beck bubbling away on your left, to reach a stone bridge near the foot of Aira Force. Cross the bridge and climb to a higher bridge where you will find a splendid view of the falls.

Continue across this bridge and turn left, with a fence on your right. When the fence ends, turn right and climb steps to a stepstile over a fence. Cross this

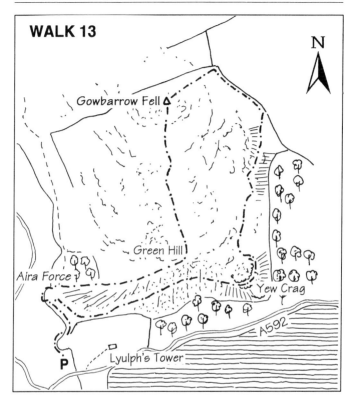

WALK 13

N

Gowbarrow Fell △

Green Hill

Aira Force

Yew Crag

A592

P

Lyulph's Tower

stile and follow the ensuing path, curving gradually up to the right between rocky outcrops.

These rocky outcrops prove to be a series of false summits, but your objective is Green Hill. When the path forks head for a rounded summit, to the left, but before reaching this the path veers, right, and heads for a double-topped summit. Go to this.

The view is already impressive. Looking back over Aira Force you can pick out the flat top of Helvellyn, and to the right rise the folds and domes of the Dodds, fine, striding country, but confusing in mist.

Leave the double-topped summit, and follow a path undulating towards a cairn, prominent on the skyline. Head for this, and press on to yet another rise, which this time proves to be the summit of Green Hill.

Once again, the view is outstanding, and reaches as far as the highest summit of the Pennines, *Cross Fell. To the north lies your next objective, Gowbarrow Fell, on which you can pick out its trig pillar. Behind it, rises the sprawling dome of Great Mell Fell.*

The onward route for Gowbarrow Fell is not always clear, and should not be attempted if you are unable to see your target all the time. Otherwise, make what you can of an indistinct path, wandering in and out of rocky, heather-mantled hollows and outcrops. A steady plod soon brings the summit beneath your feet; with it comes a splendid view and cause for a short break.

THE WAY BACK:

Not far from the summit trig you will see a wall that runs in an east-northeasterly direction, down to a wall junction. Head for this.

As you approach the wall junction, the path swings to the right into a grassy ravine, with a stream on your left. Follow this, and stay with the path, improving as it goes, until it reaches the ruins of a shooting lodge.

Go past the ruins to join a more prominent path, turning right along it, to begin a splendid traverse above the steep drop to Ullswater's shore.

Shortly after the shooting lodge the path crosses a deep gill, and later rounds a rocky corner before crossing another gill. Some stabilisation work has been carried out on this stretch, and young children will need close control.

When the path divides, take the left path, dropping a little before climbing once more and swinging right, around a corner. Ignore a steep, cairned path that drops away to your left, and continue to another corner with the top of Yew Crag now in view slightly below and to your left.

Follow the on-going path, heading down to a path junction not far from Lyulph's Tower, seen among the trees below. Ignore a gate on your left, and then bear right towards another gate, beyond which, keep left to a stile in a fence corner. A short way further on you rejoin the Aira Force footpath, to retrace your steps to the car park.

Dorothy Wordsworth's Gowbarrow Daffodils

"I never saw daffodils so beautiful, they grew among the mossy stones...some rested their heads upon these stones as on a pillow for weariness...they looked so gay ever glancing ever changing." *Thursday, 15th April 1802.*

WALK 14:
Gowbarrow Fell circuit

The delights of Aira Force are renowned and revered among those who enjoy seeking out waterfalls, and holds its place along with the many others of Lakeland. It lies within the Gowbarrow Park estate,

> **Start:** Aira Force car park. GR 401201
> **Total Distance:** 13km (8 miles)
> **Height gain:** 395m (1295 feet)
> **Difficulty:** Moderate: some steep walking near Aira Force, open country and quiet single track back roads, finishing with a lofty and airy traverse through Swinburn's Park

a medieval deer park, developed later by the Victorians and planted with Douglas firs, Chilean pine (monkey puzzle) and other exotic trees and shrubs, including many rhododendrons. In spite of that, stretches of moorland and rock, dotted with a few gnarled oak trees, still retain an impression of what it would have been like in years gone by.

Nor can any amount of artificial cloaking in alien species camouflage the dale's glacial shaping. For the Victorian visitors, the expansive views of Ullswater and the surrounding fells, crowding in on one another, were unrivalled in Lakeland.

The walk that follows first visits Aira Force, and then begins an extended version of the preceding walk, making use of popular paths and quiet back roads.

THE WALK:

Leave the car park by a gate at its northern end, and follow the path to another gate. Go right, descending through woodland, to a wooden footbridge across Aira Beck, flowing through a deep ravine. Climb a flight of steps on the opposite bank, and when the path divides, take the lower branch.

In places the path is close to a steep drop to the beck below, so very young children will need keeping in check for a while.

Go down to a stone bridge, from which there is a spectacular view of Aira Force. Once across the bridge, climb more steps at the top of which you join another path, bearing right to cross a higher bridge.

Back on the east (true left) bank, follow the left hand path above the falls, and ignore any paths going off to higher levels.

Throughout all of this section, the view of the falls, and *the scenery and landscape it has created, are fascinating and very attractive. Even the two stone bridges are constructed in differing styles: the lower is composed of vertical stones,*

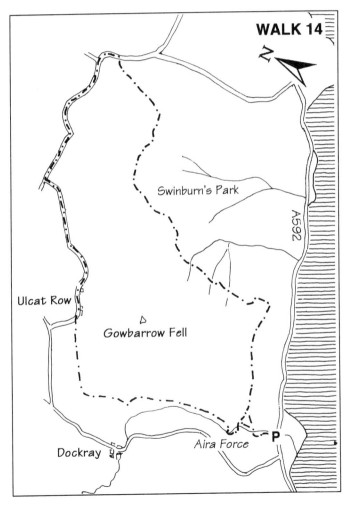

not the traditional method for these parts, while the higher bridge has horizontal stonework, more in keeping with the locality - some Victorian stonemason trying to illustrate a point, perhaps?

Keeping to the path through predominantly oak woodland, you gradually approach a higher waterfall, High Force. As you do, look for a gate bearing a notice, 'Footpath to Dockray and Ulcat Row'.

Follow this footpath, through thinning woodland, past a wall and on to open bracken heath, until you reach a faint track above a wall (signposted: Ulcat Row), that leads on through another gate, and changes direction as it passes round the crags at the northwestern extremity of Gowbarrow Fell to head northeast to meet the back road at a gate, near Ulcat Row.

Now walk, ahead, along the road, a delightful, virtually traffic-free, proposition, continuing to a T-junction. Here, turn right, as if bound for Watermillock. Regrettably, the next stage, albeit a short one, is uphill, to The Hause, a neat col, directly beneath the slopes of Little Mell Fell.

From the col go down the road, ignoring a left turn to Bennethead and Dacre. As you descend, so an escarpment develops above you on the right, Priest's Crag. Your onward route lies across the base of Priest's Crag, reached by a gate at the side of the road.

The path rises gradually to a col near Gate Crags, and directly above Hagg Wood. Continue rising with the path, passing through a gate and on below Little Meldrum.

With minor undulations the onward path is more or less level, and becomes muddy in places.

At a wall you enter the National Trust property of Gowbarrow Park, near the ruins of a shooting lodge. Climb slightly to cross three streams all making their way down to Collierhagg Beck.

Gradually the path heads for Yew Crag (sharing the rest of the journey with the preceding walk).

Beyond Yew Crag, follow the on-going path, heading down to a path junction not far from Lyulph's Tower, seen among the trees below. Ignore a gate on your left, and then bear right towards another gate, beyond which, keep left to a stile in a fence corner. A short way further on you rejoin the Aira Force footpath, to retrace your steps to the car park.

WALK 15:
The Eamont Valley

What flows into Ullswater at one end as Goldrill Beck, flows out at the other, eight or so miles later, as the River Eamont. As it does, so it passes into more pastoral, less rugged scenery, but a no less endearing landscape. Whether by this stage you consider yourself still to be in Patterdale is almost academic. For convenience sake, I take the view that the pre-glacial river beneath what is now Ullswater was Goldrill Beck,

Start: National Park Information Centre, Pooley Bridge. GR 471244
Total Distance: 8km (5 miles)
Height gain: 90m (295 feet)
Difficulty: Easy, but muddy in places

since concensus has the Eamont starting at Pooley Bridge. No one argues that the stretch of the dale where Goldrill Beck rises is Patterdale, so, the whole of the valley, up to Pooley Bridge must also be Patterdale.

The village of Pooley Bridge lies on what used to be the Westmorland side of the bridge from which it gets part of its name. 'Pooley' stands for the 'hill or mound by the pool', and refers to the thickly-wooded hill west of the village, commonly known as Dunmallet, but on some maps known as Dunmallard Hill. Such prominence, and its strategic position at a major entrance to the dale, not surprisingly attracted prehistoric interest.

The following walk is a pleasant stroll, visiting Dalmain House and Dacre Castle, starting along the banks of the River Eamont.

THE WALK:

From the Information Centre follow the main road to cross the bridge. Turn right in front of Dunmallet Hill, and go through a car park, continuing on a footpath alongside the River Eamont. A few hundred yards further on go through a gate to enter a field. Stay parallel with the river, on a grassy path, and go through a succession of gates. Near a small tarn the path turns left to reach a stile a short distance away, near a farm gate. Keeping to the field margin, go across a series of raised planks to reach the main road (A592).

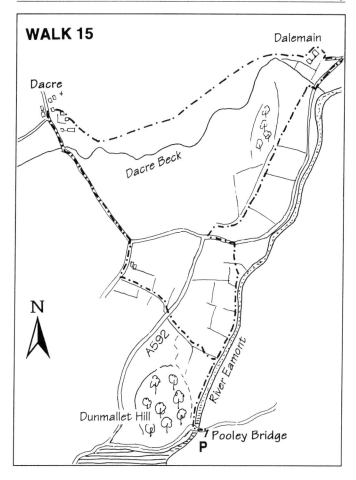

WALK 15

Dalemain

Dacre

Dacre Beck

N

A592

River Eamont

Dunmallet Hill

Pooley Bridge

P

Turn left, along the road for 200 yards, and then right (near a road junction) over a stone stile (signposted: Public Footpath). Trend right and across a field to a stile, and from there continue ahead, gradually ascending along a rutted farm track with a wire fence on your left.

Following a succession of fields and stiles, always heading in the same direction, at last you cross a final field to descend to a stone bridge, Dacre Bridge, spanning Dacre

Beck, with Dalemain House directly beyond.

Immediately before the bridge, turn right, and go over a stile to rejoin the main road. Turn left, and after about 250 yards, turn left again on to the driveway leading to Dalemain House.

Continue up the driveway, and just after you reach a car parking area on your right, go left over a cattle grid, along the rear of a barn, and enter the courtyard of the House.

Turn right, and start moving away from the House, along a stony track, with a high wall on your left. When the track levels out, it heads across open countryside all the way to Dacre Castle - a splendid interlude of invigorating walking.

Not long after reaching the castle, the track ends in the centre of Dacre village. Turn left, and follow the lane, recrossing Dacre Beck, keeping on, beyond the bridge, for another half mile to a road junction on the right (signposted: Soulby).

Turn down this road, go past a farm, and soon, at a stile, gain a bridleway entering a field on your left. Follow a wire fence, once more to reach the A592. Cross the road, and a stile (signposted: Pooley Bridge).

Keeping a hedge on your right, with the rise of Dunmallet Hill close by, climb easily to a stile, next to a gate. Shortly, go past a wooden gate, and keep on to a stile by means of which you can turn right, into an adjoining field. Once over the stile, go left, descending a grassy path back towards the River Eamont, where you rejoin the outward route.

Turn right to return to Pooley Bridge.

ALONG THE WAY:

Dacre Castle: Dacre Castle was the chief stronghold of the Dacres, and played a significant part in the history of Cumberland, being much-used during the times of the Border troubles. It dates from the fourteenth-century, and has a square tower with large turrets at the angles, and was altered in the seventeenth-century.

Dunmallet Hill is a prominent landmark at the northern end of Ullswater, and, as such, was used as an Iron Age or Romano-British settlement, the remains of which are still visible.

There is some evidence, mainly surface finds of perforated stone battle-axes, to support the view that the site was also used by the Beaker people, who reached Britain from the North European Plain around 2000 BC.

WALK 16:
Hallin Fell

One might be forgiven for assuming that its position, however prominent and inviting, on the eastern shore of Ullswater, makes Hallin Fell inaccessible to walkers: nothing could be further from

Start: Quarry car park, opposite St Peter's Church, Howtown. GR 435193
Total Distance: 5km (3 miles)
Height gain: 285m (935 feet)
Difficulty: Easy

the truth. This modest fell lies in a delectable corner of Lakeland, amid outstanding scenery that will enthral minds, young and old alike.

This walk makes a circular tour of the fell, on pleasant lakeshore paths, and climbs to its top, which is crowned by a well-constructed cairn. Of only modest duration, the walk may be combined with Walk 17, to give a longer day.

The key to the ascent is the village of Howtown, reached from Pooley Bridge by a narrow backroad, or, for sea-faring walkers, by the summer lake steamers that operate between Glenridding and Howtown. But do be sure to check the return times, or you will be faced with the long walk back to Glenridding, described in Walk 6 - which, of course, you could plan to do anyway, quite an outstanding prospect, and one of the finest low-level walks you will find in Lakeland.

THE WALK:
From the left hand end of the quarry, seek out a grassy path, now much-trampled, and ascend slightly to a wall corner. Turn right, and pursue indistinct pathways through bracken alongside a wall. Soon the wall heads downhill, but is replaced a short way ahead by another wall: between the two is a more distinct

path ascending from the left, which you now follow, to go along a wall, and gradually down into trees and a junction with the lakeshore path near Sandwick Bay and a gate.

Turn right and follow the path, ignoring diversions. The path emerges from the woodland near Kailpot Crag, a small rocky headland, and starts to slant to the right, and to climb to reach the topside of a wall, overlooking Howtown Bay.

Ignore a gate in the wall, staying above the wall, and when, later, the path forks, take the right branch, a broad grassy track, climbing steadily uphill above the Howtown zigzags (a motorist's nightmare) to return to the car park.

Having walked all the way round the fell, you might as well now take the obvious, wide, grassy path from the car park that climbs to the top - after all, I've allowed for it in the distance and height gain.

The 12-foot high obelisk that stands on the grassy, brackeny, knolly, top of the fell is a massive structure of squared stones. Numerous paltry attempts to emulate it are scattered about: one or two are sited strategically, and command views of Ullswater, Martindale, and the fells across the lake that quite simply are breathtaking.

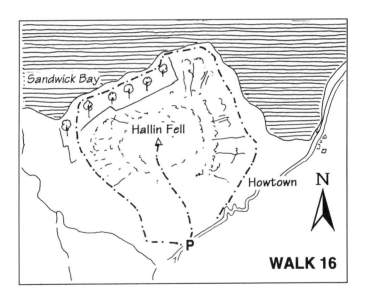

WALK 17:
Pikewassa

A number of valleys feed down to the lakeside communities of Sandwick and Howtown from the vast area known as Martindale. Few of them are known outside the immediate locality; Boardale, was visited on Walk 6, but nearby lies the valley in which lies the

---

Start: Quarry car park, opposite St Peter's Church, Howtown. GR 435193
Total Distance: 5km (3 miles)
Height gain: 205m (670feet)
Difficulty: Easy

---

village of Martindale itself, dividing in its upper reaches into Bannerdale and Ramps Gill - delightful dales, but into which there is limited access. Even smaller, is Fusedale, sandwiched between the objective of this walk, Pikewassa, and the much higher Loadpot Hill at the northern end of the High Street range of fells.

The modest proportions of Pikewassa nevertheless conceal a fine summital ridge and rocky summit from which to survey the recesses of Martindale and Fusedale. When Hallin Fell and the Ullswater lakeshore paths are crowded in summer, Pikewassa will be less so, and more certain to afford quiet spots in which to relax and enjoy a felltop picnic. It is a good place, too, from which to begin teaching young children about map-reading, and, in particular, how to orientate the map with the landscape.

THE WALK:

From the car park head for nearby St Peter's Church, and go alongside a wall to reach diminutive Lanty Tarn.

Turn left, and pursue a grassy path slanting gently down the fellside. After a while a wall ascends from the left to accompany the path. When it does, start looking for a a small manhole cover in the path, near a stone marker, just before you reach a rocky outcrop on the right.

Go right here, climbing the bank above the path to reach a grassy ledge. Follow a narrow path climbing steeply to the right of some rocks. As you ascend, so the path improves, and a few cairns start to appear, leading on to the crest of a delightfully rocky ridge.

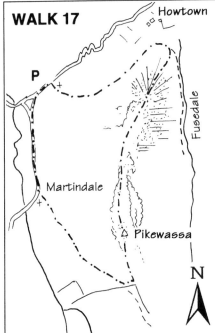

WALK 17

Howtown

P

Martindale

△ Pikewassa

Fusedale

N

shapely peak of The Nab is set against the higher mound of Rest Dod, while to the east, across Fusedale, rises the long, grassy ridge extending north-wards from High Raise to Loadpot Hill.

Continue along the ridge until finally you reach the rocky summit of Pikewassa.

THE WAY BACK:

Follow the on-going path across the summit, and go down to a gap in a wall. Turn right and go down, steeply, alongside a wall to reach a lower path.

The retrospective view of Ullswater is especially pleasing from this end of the ridge, and a good excuse to pause for a breather.

As you press on along the ridge, the angle eases, the ridge becomes wider, and the view more impressive with virtually every stride.

Place Fell is unavoidably obvious across the deep troughs of Martindale and Boardale, while across Boardale Hause you can pick out the shapely top of St Sunday Crag, with Fairfield beyond. Nearer to hand, the

Down in Martindale below you is The Bungalow, former shooting lodge of the Earls of Lonsdale, and where the Kaiser Wilhelm II stayed prior to the First World War.

Martindale is also renowned for some, now remnants, of the oldest relict or native woodland in the Lake District.

Turn right along the lower path to reach the rear of St Martin's Church.

Now follow the quiet road back to the car park at Howtown.

GENERAL INFORMATION
AND
USEFUL ADDRESSES

LAKE DISTRICT NATIONAL PARK

The Lake District National Park is the local government body established in 1951 to preserve and enhance the beauty of the area, and to promote quiet public enjoyment and understanding. At 885 square miles, the Lake District is the largest of the national parks throughout England and Wales.

Contrary to popular belief, much of the land in the national park is privately-owned, and the National Park Authority works closely with landowners to ensure that the 1800 miles of footpath is accessible both to the local population, and the annual influx of visitors.

Visitor information about any part of the national park, together with an accommodation booking service, informative exhibitions, free information, and a comprehensive range of guidebooks and maps, are available from the Tourist Information Centre, situated in Glenridding. The centre is open daily from 10.00 am to 5.00 pm from 1 April to 3 November (or thereabouts), with some extension of opening hours during the summer months.

Lake District National Park Office, Murley Moss,
Oxenholme Road, KENDAL, Cumbria, LA9 7RL
Tel 0539 724555: Fax 0539 740822

CUMBRIA TOURIST BOARD

The Cumbria Tourist Board exists to guide the development of the tourism industry in Cumbria, to bring economic, social and environment benefits to the region. It operates an accommodation service, and a number of Tourist Information Centres, some of which have a free local accommodation booking service, or a nationwide 'Book-a-Bed-Ahead' service.

Cumbria Tourist Board, Ashleigh, Holly Road,
WINDERMERE, Cumbria, LA23 2AQ
Tel 05394 44444

WHERE TO STAY

The scope for overnight accommodation anywhere in the Lake District is enormous. All the main towns and villages within reasonable travelling distance of Patterdale - Penrith, Pooley Bridge, Glenridding, Patterdale itself, and Ambleside - have plentiful bed and breakfast accommodation ranging from private houses to hotels and guest houses of a high standard, while virtually every village and many of the farms have some bed and breakfast accommodation. Wherever you go, you will be assured of a warm and friendly welcome.

There are many camping and caravan sites, and these are shown on the various maps that are available. Members of the Youth Hostels Association will find youth hostels at Greenside, and Patterdale, both conveniently situated for the walks contained in this guide. Those who are not members may like to join. Write to:

Youth Hostels Association National Office
Trevelyan House, 8 St Stephen's Hill,
ST ALBANS, Hertfordshire, AL1 2DY

or

YHA Northern England Regional Office
PO Box 11, MATLOCK, Derbyshire

LAKE DISTRICT WEATHER

In the Lake District the weather is often very much a law unto itself. The months from April until July tend to be the driest of the year, while autumn quite often proves an excellent time of year for walking. By the time September and October arrive, you could encounter the occasional flurry of snow, or a chilling wind, but you are just as likely to have prolonged periods of calm and a serene stillness for which the Lake District is renowned. You can get local weather reports from a few places. Weather bulletins are usually posted at national park car parks and tourist information centres. Or you can ring -

Lake District Weather Service
05394 45151